Walking Toward the Sacred:
Our Great Lakes Tobacco Story

Compiled and Edited by
Isaiah Brokenleg and Elizabeth Tornes

Design and Layout by
Nakota Designs
www.nakotadesigns.com

Great Lakes Inter-Tribal Epidemiology Center
PO Box 9
Lac du Flambeau, WI 54538
www.glitc.org/epicenter/

ISBN: 978-1-4675-6122-8

First Printing in the United States.

Printed by
Hahn Printing, Incorporated
752 North Adams Rd.
Eagle River, Wisconsin 54521
www.hahnprinting.com

*This book is dedicated to our future generations and the elders
who shared their wisdom and stories with us.*

Acknowledgements

The editors would like to thank the many people and organizations who helped to make this possible:

The CPPW Tribal Contributors: Mark Caskey, Carol "Bruiser" Gordon, Elizabeth Hagen, Janet Hillert, Lenore "Pumpkin" Shepherd, and Becky Taylor

The Late Delores "Dee" DePerry Bainbridge

Teresa K. Barber," Kaw^nokwas" (Oneida), "Awaanibiisaa-Giizhigookwe" (Ojibwe)

Steve Busalacchi

Joe Chosa, "Ozaawaabik"

Zachary "Sho Nuff" Harris

Jim Pete, "Guyaushk"

The Late Eddie Roy

Wayne Valliere, "Minogiizhig"

The Communities Putting Prevention to Work (CPPW) Partnering Tribes: Lac Courte Oreilles Band of Ojibwe, Menominee Indian Tribe of Wisconsin, Red Cliff Band of Lake Superior Chippewa, St. Croix Chippewa Indians of Wisconsin, and the Stockbridge-Munsee Community Band of Mohican Indians

The Centers for Disease Control and Prevention

Cherokee Nation

College of the Menominee Nation

Cultural Wellness Center (previously Powderhorn Phillips Cultural Wellness Center)

Great Lakes Inter-Tribal Council

Health First Wisconsin

Nakota Designs

Oneida Nation of Wisconsin

The Tobacco Prevention and Control Program of Wisconsin

Turtle Mountain Chippewa Historical Society

Wisconsin Clearinghouse for Prevention

The Wisconsin Native American Tobacco Network

Walking Toward the Sacred: Our Great Lakes Tobacco Story
was made possible thanks to a grant from the Centers for Disease Control and Prevention, Communities Putting Prevention to Work Program.

TABLE OF CONTENTS

Walking Toward the Sacred:
Our Great Lakes Tobacco Story

INTRODUCTION
By Isaiah Brokenleg, Sicangu Lakota
Director of the Communities Putting Prevention to Work Project
at Great Lakes Inter-Tribal Council

The impetus for this project grew out of a need for education about traditional tobacco. Many people from within our culture and those outside of our culture do not know about traditional tobacco and the differences between traditional tobacco and commercial tobacco. In our efforts to create a society and culture free from the harms of commercial tobacco, we encounter many American Indians who think that commercial tobacco is the same tobacco that was used for ceremony centuries ago. We also encounter many non-Indians who are ignorant about American Indian ceremonial tobacco use, and do not understand why any tobacco control efforts in Indian Country must honor ceremonial tobacco use if they are to be effective.

In 2010, the Great Lakes Inter-Tribal Council received a Communities Putting Prevention to Work (CPPW) grant from the Centers for Disease Control and Prevention to work on tobacco control with five Wisconsin Tribes who chose to participate: Lac Courte Oreilles Band of Ojibwe, the Menominee Indian Tribe of Wisconsin, the Red Cliff Band of Lake Superior Chippewa, the St. Croix Chippewa Indians of Wisconsin, and the Stockbridge-Munsee Community Band of Mohican Indians. CPPW partnered with the Wisconsin Native American Tobacco Network, a coalition of the eleven Wisconsin Tribes, to reduce commercial tobacco use and exposure while supporting ceremonial tobacco use. One of the projects we collaborated on was the creation of this traditional tobacco document.

This document contains some of our traditional tobacco stories and teachings, information on traditional (ceremonial) tobacco, differences between traditional tobacco and commercial tobacco, instructions on how to grow traditional tobacco, and information about commercial tobacco harms. We hope that you can learn from and enjoy this document.

We understand that many American Indians, for several different reasons, still use commercial tobacco for ceremonies. We wish to educate people about tobacco that was used traditionally, and do not wish to criticize or judge those who use commercial tobacco for ceremony today. We understand that commercial tobacco, unlike traditional tobacco, is often easier to access. However, many elders and spiritual leaders teach us to return to the traditional ways, using only traditional tobacco for ceremonies. Growing your own traditional tobacco is explained in this document, and will allow you to produce your own homegrown traditional tobacco.

We understand that many of the stories and teachings outlined in this book are not solely the intellectual property of the person telling the story, but are instead their versions of the stories and teachings passed down to them from earlier generations, and which they in turn share for generations to come....

Many of our communities are losing their culture, language, and stories at an alarming rate. At the same time, some communities have taboos about when stories should and should not be told, and what teachings should and should not be shared. We have tried to balance the need to preserve the culture, stories, and teachings with the need to respect and honor the protocols in our communities. We consulted many elders, spiritual leaders, and community leaders in this matter and believe the document before you honors both of these important needs.

Working with the Wisconsin Native American Network, we invited Tobacco Coordinators from all the Wisconsin Tribes to contribute stories and teachings to this collection. This document shares the stories, teachings, and culture of those who contributed to it. It reflects what we were taught, told, learned, and understand. We know that each person may have learned and may under-stand something different from what is presented here. It is not meant to represent every American Indian culture, community, or person, but rather a collection of stories and teachings from those who shared them with us.

We designed this document with two different audiences in mind. We wanted to share it with American Indians from this area in order to help educate, preserve and perpetuate our culture. We also wanted to share it with our non-Indian relatives so that they may learn about our culture and make better, more culturally informed, decisions with regard to tobacco control policy, services, and funding.

We did not design this document for those who wish to misappropriate or commodify our culture. We hope that you will not use the information contained within it to misappropriate, commodify or commercialize American Indian stories, teachings, or culture.

As only the Creator is perfect, we do not seek perfection in this document, but instead seek to provide something that benefits our communities and helps us to be healthy.

Tobacco's Past

TOBACCO STORIES AND TEACHINGS

Anishinaabe Stories and Teachings

According to the Elders, there was a time when the people of the earth were not living their lives in a proper manner and the Creator decided that he was going to do away with them. But, the eagle interceded on the human's behalf.

The Creator said as long as there is still one person who lives their life in a correct way with Asema (tobacco), the humans would be spared.

So each morning the eagle goes out and flies over the earth to see if we live our lives in the correct way. As long as he sees that Indian people still use their tobacco and still use their language and follow the old ways, we will be all right.

In the old days, it was easy to see where the Indian people were, but today with houses and buildings, it is not quite so easy. So one of the things we do is put up a Spirit Pole. This pole lets the Spirit World know that we are living our lives in a correct manner, with respect.

Using the left hand when holding tobacco is encouraged, because the left hand is closest to the heart.

— Based on the traditions of the Anishinaabe Elders, this Wenaboozhoo story on the creation of tobacco was shared by Jim Pete, Red Cliff Tribal member.

"Gichi mewinzha, Wenaboozhoo izhinikaazo, gii-pii-miinogod Anishinaabe asema omaa akiing. Mino ezhichigewaad, gii-ikido Wenaboozhoo, igiw Anishinaabeg. Noongom, gaawiin noondawaasiin a'aw Wenaboozhoo. Mii dash weweni aakoziiwag miziwe Anishinaabeg aaking noongom. Gaawiin noondawaasiin a'aw Wenaboozhoo."

"A long time ago, our great uncle Wenaboozhoo[1], as he is called, gave Native people here on earth tobacco. He told them to use it in a good way. Because we didn't listen, and we are not listening to what the Great Spirit's son Wenaboozhoo told us a long time ago, about how sacred tobacco is, because we didn't listen to that, our people have become sick from it, and our people are dying from it. Hopefully one day we'll be able to listen again, and our people will have mino-ayaawin, which is good health. Mii etawa ekidoyan, that's all I have."

— Excerpt from an interview by Steve Busalacchi with Wayne "Minogiizhig" Valliere, Lac du Flambeau Tribal Member and Ojibwe Language and Culture Instructor for the Lac du Flambeau Tribe, in January 2012

— Opwaagan (pipe) made by Wayne "Minogiizhig" Valliere. Photo by Gisele Zenti.

---

[1]Wenaboozhoo (also known by a variety of other names and spellings, including Wenabojo, Menabozho, and Nanabush) is a trickster figure and culture hero, the protagonist of many Anishinaabe origin stories.

Mashkiki (Medicine)

Tobacco is the first plant that the Creator gave to the Anishinaabe people. Three other plants: sage, cedar and sweet grass are [also] held sacred by the people. Together they are referred to as the four sacred medicines (Mashkiki). The four sacred medicines are used in everyday life and in all of our ceremonies. All of them can be used to smudge with, though sage, cedar, and sweet grass also have many other uses. It is said that tobacco sits in the eastern door, sweet grass in the southern door, sage in the west, and cedar in the north. Elders say that the spirits like the aroma produced when the other sacred medicines are burned. *This information on "Mashkiki" is from the Turtle Mountain Chippewa Historical Society website; content is provided by Kade M. Ferris, M.S.*

Asema - Waabanong (East)

Sacred tobacco (spelled Asema or Asemaa) was given to the Anishinaabe so that we can communicate with the Spirit world. Tobacco is always offered before picking other medicines. When you offer tobacco to a plant and explain your reasons for being there, the plant will let all the plants in the area know your intentions and why you are picking them. Tobacco is used as an offering, a gift, and is an important part of Anishinaabe ceremonies.

Wiingashk - Zhaawanong (South)

Sweet grass is the sacred hair of Mother Earth. Its sweet aroma reminds our people of the gentleness, love, and kindness she has for the people. When sweet grass is used in a healing circle it has a calming effect. Like sage and cedar, sweet grass is used for smudging and purification.

Mashkodewashk - Ningabii-anong (West)

Sage is used to prepare our people for ceremonies and teachings. Because it is more medicinal and stronger than sweet grass, sage is used more often in ceremonies. Sage is used for releasing what is troubling the mind and for removing negative energy. It is also used for cleansing homes and in sacred bundles carried by people. It also has other medicinal uses.

Giizhik - Giiwedinong (North)

Like sage and sweet grass, cedar is used to purify the home; it also has many restorative medicinal uses. When mixed with sage for a tea, it cleans the body of all infections, cedar baths are also very healing. When cedar, mixed with tobacco, is put in the fire it crackles, this is said to call the attention of the Spirits (Manidoog) to the offering that is being made. Cedar is used in sweat lodge and fasting ceremonies for protection, cedar branches cover the floor of many sweat lodges and some people make a circle of cedar when they are fasting. It is a guardian spirit and chases away the bad spirits.

"Asema is red willow." --Jim Pete

The following information was submitted from Jim Pete, Red Cliff Tribal member, whose Indian name is Guyaushk (Seagull). Jim indicated it was such an honor to be asked to contribute the information about asema (tobacco) from Red Cliff. He stated he learned this as a young boy, growing up in Red Cliff, from a couple of elders who wanted to pass on the traditions of asema from the Red Cliff community aspect.

Eddie Roy was an elder who taught Jim about using the red willow branches and bark in making asema. He said, "Eddie showed me the red willow on the sides of the roads and how it was collected. He also showed me how to lightly scrape the red willow bark off the branches and if possible, to let them dry. Eddie said to also lightly scrape off the part right under the bark, and this is what we used to use for our tobacco." If it is dried naturally, it can be smoked like that. However, it can also be put in a pan and roasted in the oven for a bit, or put in a cast iron skillet and roasted that way. He was advised to turn the shavings, so they do not scorch or burn.

Another elder who taught many people about the use of asema was Delores DePerry Bainbridge. Dee was raised by her grandparents, where Anishinaabemowin was their first language. "Dee would teach us many things about the language, how to prepare wild game, and the use of asema. Dee said as a young girl she wanted to go

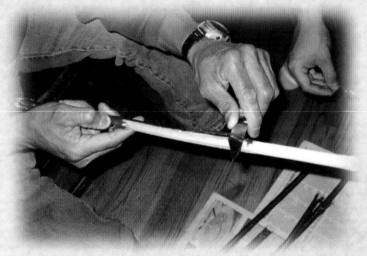

Miskwaabiimizh (Red Willow) Photo by Ivy Vainio

out and play with her friends, but her Gramma would make her stay in the house and talk Indian to her, to teach her. In those teachings were the various stories about Wenaboozhoo and how he helped the Anishinaabe learn about life. He was sometimes very wise and sometimes very foolish."

Dee would tell the story about how asema was given to the Anishinaabe, from the red willow. As Jim thought of this contribution, part of his journey was remembering the teachings of Eddie Roy and Dee Bainbridge. A part of this journey was also trying to find that common ground, so as to not offend anyone in sharing the Wenaboozhoo story. He acknowledged how there are limitations in which to share things, based on traditional teachings.

Anishinaabe Aadizooke
(S/he Tells a Sacred Indian Story)

"When Wenaboozhoo awoke, he was very hungry and started to take out his goslings from the fire. But he could find nothing buried in the ashes. He was furious with his buttocks and decided to punish them by standing over the fire until they were scorched. At last, when the buttocks were black and crisp, Wenaboozhoo tried to walk away, but it was so painful that he could scarcely move. So he sat on the top of a steep cliff and slid down, and the sore skin of his buttocks ended up on the shrubs. As he walked along, he dragged his bleeding buttocks behind him through some dense shrubs. When he looked back, the shrubs were red from his blood. This, said Wenaboozhoo, will be what the people will use to mix their tobacco--the red willows."

— by Dee Bainbridge, as told to Jim Pete. Jim said with all due respect to all the other considerations, he wanted to share these contributions with the hope they will also teach and inspire others to remember, honor, and respect the teachings of our Elders.

Menominee Tobacco Story

An early Menominee legend tells how tobacco was given to Ma-Na-Bus who stole it from a mountain giant. Ma-Na-Bus had smelled the delightful odor and asked the giant to give him some. The giant told him the spirits had been there smoking during their annual ceremony. He told Ma-Na-Bus to come back in a year and he might ask them for some tobacco as he had none himself. But Ma-Na-Bus spied dozens of bags filled with tobacco and immediately snatched up one. Then he ran off to the mountaintop. He was pursued so closely by the giant that only by trickery did he succeed in defending himself. He threw the giant down to the ground, crying "because you are so wicked you shall be known as Jumper the grasshopper. By your stained mouth everyone will know you. You will be the enemy of those agriculture men who raise tobacco!" Then Ma-Na-Bus divided the tobacco among his brothers and in the way it was finally delivered to the Indians. Accounts show that even today the grasshopper shoots tobacco juice from its mouth.

— By a Menominee Elder, from a framed quote at the College of the Menominee Nation. Submitted by Mark Caskey, Menominee Nation Wellness Director.

Oneida Creation Story –
How Tobacco Was Created*

The excerpt below is from the Oneida Nation of Wisconsin's website, "The Creation Story:"

This is one of many versions of the Oneida Creation Story. The Iroquois people all have their own similar, yet different version of how creation started.

"Long ago, before there was any land here, there was water all over, the only things were the creatures that lived in the water and the birds that flew above the waters. Now further above there was land which was called the Sky World and there were beings living there, and these beings had supernatural powers. In the middle of the land was a great tree which gave them their light. There were many different things that grew on the tree; this is where they retrieved things to sustain their lives.

Now, it was that no one could cut into the tree or a great punishment would be given to that person, whoever was caught harming the tree. There was this couple and the young woman was to have a baby. This woman started to crave things and one of the things she craved was the roots and bark from the tree, so she asked her husband to go and gather this for her. He was afraid to get these items because he would surely be punished. He waited for the people to go from the tree. As they all left he went over and started digging.

As he was digging by the tree, suddenly the ground caved in and it left a big hole. The man got very scared of what had happened, so he went back and told his wife. She asked if he got what she had wanted. He told her he did not because he had gotten so scared. She was very upset and said she would get it herself.

As she arrived at to the tree, she saw the hole and went over to get a closer look. As she was looking through, she saw all the water down below. She did not know that her husband followed her. As she was looking through the hole, she slipped and fell. As she was falling she tried to grab hold of something so she would not fall. All she could grab was some of the ground and roots of the tree, but she could not hold on and she fell through. As she fell, the birds and water animals saw the light through the hole and they could see something falling. The birds were appointed to see what was falling and they found that it was a woman from the Sky World.

They sent one of the birds back down to the water animals to see which one of them would able to support her upon their back. After they talked amongst themselves to see who would be able to support her. They turned to the great turtle and she agreed to support the woman. The birds went up to bring the woman down safely and placed her on the turtle's back.

As the woman was falling she got very frightened and fainted. She awoke on the turtle's back and all she saw was water, the birds and the water animals. She asked where she was and the animals told her that she fell through a hole and they put her on turtle's back. She looked to where they had pointed and to see the light shining through the hole.

She asked the animals if they knew where there would be any mud or dirt so she could mix it with the medicines she had grabbed as she fell through the hole. Some of the animals said they were not sure but there might be some at the bottom of the water.

First, the otter said he would go down and see if there was any, then he went underwater and was gone. Everyone waited patiently for the otter. Soon he came floating to the top, but didn't get any mud. So the loon said it would try and went underwater. Everyone waited patiently for the loon to come up and soon she came up and she too did not have any mud either. So the beaver said he would try and away he went. Soon he came up with none and felt very sad. The woman told him not to feel bad and that he had tried his

best. So the muskrat said he would try and he went down. For a long time, the muskrat was gone and they became worried. Then the muskrat came floating to the top with a little bit of dirt in-between his claws. The woman took it and mixed it with the medicines. She then began to rub the mixture in a counter clockwise direction and the land began to expand out.

Then the woman began to gather things, for she was getting ready to give birth to a child. As the time came, she gave birth to a girl and she was very happy. The woman and her daughter walked about the earth and she taught her about the different things that grew and what they were used for. As the days and years went by the young girl grew to womanhood and she was very beautiful. As she was walking far from her mother, there was a man that appeared before her.

The girl became terrified at seeing this man and she fainted.

As she came to, she noticed that there were these two arrows on her stomach. One had a sharp point on it and the other was dull. She took them home with her. She told her mother of this man that she had seen and of the two arrows he had left behind. Her mother explained to her that they were from sky world and that the man that came to her was the West wind and that she would have two children. Each arrow represented one of the two children.

As the days went by the young woman did not feel too good because there was a great commotion within her body. When it was finally time to give birth, the right handed twin came out first, the natural way, while the left handed twin had seen light coming from her mouth and wanted to go that way. As he went that way, he came out her side by her armpit and it killed their mother.

Right away the left handed twin spoke up and said it was the right handed twin that killed their mother. Then the right handed twin spoke up and explained to their grandmother what had happened. He told her that he and his brother were arguing about who was going to be born first. The right handed twin told his grandmother that he was going to be born the way all children are born and his brother said he was going any way he wanted to and he came out of their mother's armpit and that is what killed her. But, the grandmother did not believe the right handed twin and took the side of the left handed twin. She told the right handed twin as part of his punishment he had to bury their mother and angrily he started to bury his mother. As he finished, there immediately grew corn, squash and Indian tobacco."

Teresa K. Barber, Oneida/Chippewa, also known as Kaw^nokwas (her Oneida name) and Awaanibiisaa-Giizhigookwe (her Ojibwe name), says that Oneida people still grow tobacco. The Oneida Nation's Tsyunhehkwa Organic Farm grows tobacco, among other crops, and provides it to tribal members, but does not sell it. Ojibwe people also grow it for ceremonial purposes, she says, and several Ojibwe reservations have different entities that grow it, as well as individuals.

(*story used with permission)

Traditional Tobacco History

Prior to colonization, American Indians had an intimate knowledge of the world around them. This included animals, geography, and plants. Some plants were used for food, others for housing or making tools, and some were used as physical or spiritual medicines. Tobacco is one such plant that was used as a medicine. Tobacco came to American Indians a very long time ago. Each community has a story about how tobacco has come to them. We have included some of those stories in this document.

Prior to colonization, in the Great Lakes area, the plants used by themselves or in combination to make tobacco were *Nicotiana rustica* (traditional tobacco), red willow tree bark, sage, sweet grass, cedar and other botanicals. Since colonization, and with it the commercialization of tobacco, there has been a shift in the type of tobacco used by Native people. Many American Indians substitute *Nicotiana tabacum* (commercial tobacco) for the original *N. rustica* (traditional tobacco) (American Lung Association, 2004; Struthers &

Hodge, 2004). This shift may be partly caused by the ease of access to commercial tobacco. Part of this shift may also have started during the time when it was illegal for American Indians to practice their spirituality. The American Indian Community Tobacco Project (AICTP) reports that, "It is believed that the need to conduct ceremonies in secret and begin using commercial tobacco to, 'hide in plain sight,' was a factor in the inculcation of commercial tobacco into American Indian cultures in this region" (American Indian Community Tobacco Project, 2006). It was not until the passage of The Indian Religious Freedom Act of 1978 that American Indians were allowed to use tobacco legally in ceremonies.

Since the shift toward using commercial tobacco in ceremonies occurred, many young people have grown up seeing commercial tobacco being used in ceremonies and do not know the history. This perpetuates the use of commercial tobacco use in ceremony and lack of understanding regarding what is traditional tobacco, access to traditional tobacco, and cultivation of traditional tobacco.

Differences Between Traditional and Commercial Tobacco

Each culture has its own word for tobacco and some have several words. In some cultures this word describes only the tobacco plant, *Nicotiana rustica* or *Nicotiana tabacum*. For others, it can be a mixture of *N. rustica* with other botanicals such as cedar, the bark of the red willow, sweet grass, or sage. In some cases, the "tobacco" may not contain any tobacco at all. In many languages, the word for commercial tobacco and traditional tobacco is the same word. Further, in some languages the word for cigarette and tobacco is the same word. This can make it difficult to educate about the differences between commercial tobacco and the tobacco we used a long time ago. (McGaa, 1990; Struthers & Hodge, 2004; Winter, 2000)

Commercial Tobacco

Commercial tobacco is the tobacco that is sold in stores and used for cigarettes, cigars, spit tobacco, and packaged pipe tobacco. Commercial tobacco is sometimes also known by its scientific name, *Nicotiana tabacum*. Commercial tobacco is indigenous to southern North America, Central America, and the Caribbean. Commercial tobacco grows very tall, usually over five feet. The flowers on commercial tobacco are white with pink or purple tips and resemble a trumpet or horn. The leaves, which vary in size, are largest at the bottom and smaller at the top with the largest leaves growing to be about two feet long. The leaves of commercial tobacco are narrower than the leaves of traditional tobacco.

Traditional Tobacco

Traditional tobacco, also known by its scientific name, *Nicotiana rustica*, is one of the plants used alone or in combination as traditional tobacco. *N. rustica* is indigenous to many areas all over the world including the Great Lakes region. *N. rustica* grows to a maximum height of about three feet. The flowers on *N. rustica* are shaped like those on commercial tobacco. However, they are yellow. The leaves also vary in size with the largest being on the bottom and the smallest on top. However, the leaves of *N. rustica* reach a maximum length of about nine inches and are wider than those of commercial tobacco. Finally, *N. rustica* has four to 15 times the nicotine content of commercial tobacco, which could explain why traditional tobacco is not usually inhaled when smoked in a pipe.

Tobacco's Present
RESTORING TRADITION AND REDUCING HARMS

Traditional Tobacco

Nicotiana rustica is a tobacco product most often used in a traditional manner. If home grown, this product is free of the impurities added by the tobacco industry. The flowers of this plant are yellow in color. Nicotine content is highest among all other tobacco species, which is why it is not generally inhaled.

Many Tribes use other plants in their kinnickinnick (or "mixture") for smoking ceremonially. These medicines may include tobacco, cedar, sweet grass, sage, bear berry, or huckleberry bark. Some Tribes replace tobacco with willow bark or plants that are relevant for their geographical area.

Traditional Tobacco Protocol, Uses and Beliefs

Beliefs about, protocol, and uses of tobacco vary. Each Tribe varies in which way or combination of ways their people use tobacco. We encourage you to discuss tobacco protocol, beliefs, and uses specific to your community with an elder or spiritual leader. In this document, we have included common protocols for tobacco use in the Great Lakes region.

Women who are "on their moon" (menstruating) are discouraged from participating in certain ceremonies, sometimes including those where tobacco is used. This is not because women are "dirty" or "bad" during that time. In fact, the opposite is true: It is because during their moon time women are most powerful, and it is believed that their power might interfere with the balance of the ceremony.

People often take and hold tobacco in their left hand, as this is the hand closest to one's heart. As with any prayer or ceremony, it is important to not use traditional tobacco if you are under the influence of drugs or alcohol. If you make a request with tobacco, make sure to let the person or persons know your request before handing them your tobacco, so they have the right to respectively decline, if need be.

Finally, tobacco was given as gift to the people to help, heal, and walk in a good way. For this reason, it is important to never use tobacco while carrying bad thoughts in your heart or head. Likewise, our prayers should never be malicious or harmful, only positive and benevolent.

Spiritual Uses

Tobacco is used as a spiritual medicine for healing of mind, body and spirit. It is used in prayer as an offering to the Creator or other spiritual being(s). Its smoke is believed to be a medium of communication, carrying prayers to the Creator. The smoke is also used to cleanse, purify, or bless almost anything, from people to possessions. It is believed to be a great spiritual "commodity" that can be offered as a gift to honor someone, to say thank you, as a sign of respect, and to ask for prayers, advice, or favors. For example, tobacco was offered to many of the people who contributed to this. Tobacco is also used to ask for protection.

Tobacco can be smoked in a pipe. The smoke is offered to the spirits and can represent the breath of the grandfather (an expression representing ancestors or sometimes the Creator). When smoked in a pipe ceremonially, tobacco smoke is not inhaled into the lungs, but only held briefly in the mouth and exhaled. Tobacco is often held in the left hand while praying and then offered to the Creator, spirits, earth, or others by being placed near a tree, put into water, or put into a fire. Tobacco can be used to "smudge" people, places, and possessions. Smudging is the act of burning certain spiritual medicines and wafting the smoke to the areas you wish to cleanse, purify, or bless.

Tobacco is also used to make tobacco ties. A tobacco tie is a small amount of tobacco (usually just enough to load a pipe or less) wrapped in cloth and tied around the top. These ties can be single units and used when offering tobacco. In some communities, tobacco ties represent one's prayers, and each tie is connected to another in a long string of ties. It is important to not disturb tobacco ties if you happen to come across them, because they represent someone's prayer(s).

Tobacco is commonly used in spiritual ceremonies, the most obvious being the pipe ceremony. At some pipe ceremonies, only the celebrant smokes the pipe, and at others, everyone does. Each community has its own spiritual beliefs and practices. In the Great Lakes region, common spiritual traditions where tobacco is used include the Big Drum, Midewewin, the Longhouse, and the Native American Church. Tobacco is often used at ceremonies marking life transitions such as births, puberty, weddings, funerals, and memorials. It is also used when someone receives his or her spiritual or "Indian" name.

Tobacco is used as a way to ask permission or forgiveness, and to give thanks for harvesting a resource. For example, tobacco is offered when taking anything from the earth, in hunting, fishing, harvesting rice, berries, medicines and other plants. Often people will "put tobacco out" when they pass a dead animal on the road while driving, to honor that animal's spirit. Tobacco is often offered at the beginning of an event to bless it, such as a powwow, the first time someone dances, the first time dancing in particular regalia, moving into a new place, using a new car, at the beginning of a trip, before a talking circle, or at the start of a meeting. This ensures that things are done "in a good way." While this list is not exhaustive, these are some examples of how tobacco is commonly used.

Tobacco's Present

"How Do You Use Tobacco?" An Interview with Lac du Flambeau Tribal Elder Ozaawaabik (Joe Chosa)

"There are four different medicines we use: tobacco, cedar, sweet grass, and sage. Tobacco's used if you really want something, you have to give it to the person you're asking. If they accept, they have to help you out. If the person accepts, they're committed to helping you. When you take anything from the land, like if you go hunting, hunt a deer, partridge, goose, duck, anything you take from the earth, you put that tobacco down. My grandfather taught me that.

"He'd put salt in an old rotten stump, three weeks later he'd look at it—he took me one day. 'Don't move anything,' he said, 'All you move is your eyes, and no sudden movements.' We waited, we were anxious—all of a sudden a deer would sneak in through the woods, start eating that stump. He'd have us go real slow, he shot that deer, took it back into the woods. The CCC[2] Camp used to make roads, plant trees, like that farm at Arnett Road, that's what they'd do. He dropped it deeper in the woods, gutted it there. He'd cover the guts with sand and he took out a little tobacco pouch—he always had it—and said a prayer.

"When you take something like that from the land, an animal, partridge, goose, that you eat, put tobacco and give thanks for it. He always did that. When he picked something he grew, like carrots, beans, potatoes, he did that again. Don't you ever forget that. People should be thankful for what they get.

"Fishing once on a lake, he showed me a [sand] bar, and we caught six walleyes. We put tobacco in the water to give thanks for those walleyes. I wanted to stay. 'We can come back another day, get more.' I learned an important lesson that day. Don't overtake anything. Leave them so they'll reproduce.

"You go to meetings—Odanah, Lac Courte Oreilles —they always put tobacco down to start their prayer. They consider it sacred. People accept tobacco for naming ceremonies. If someone dies, they'll say prayers, or for someone who's sick. Anytime someone needs help, that's what they do. Put tobacco down. Put it next to some good strong tree.

"My grandmother raised me. When she used to see a storm approaching, like if a storm were approaching from the South, you'd see the light above the trees like flashlights and hear the rumble, she'd always take her tobacco out and say a prayer. 'Mii babaa-inaabiwaad animikiig.' That's when you see the flashing lights on the horizon but don't hear any thunder. That means that the thunderbirds are looking around. "Gego bagadiniken, gego da ezhiwebiziiyaang." Don't let anything happen to us. She was giving her prayer to the creator, to make sure you wouldn't get hurt."

---

[2]CCC or Civilian Conservation Corps (CCC) was a public work program that operated from 1933 to 1942 in the United States for unemployed, unmarried men from relief families, ages 17–23. A part of the President Franklin D. Roosevelt's New Deal, it provided unskilled manual labor jobs related to the conservation and development of natural resources in rural lands. Indian Conservation Corps (ICC) was the same type of program operating on tribal reservations.

Joe "Ozaawaabik" Chosa spoke with Beth Tornes on October 6, 2012, at his home in Lac du Flambeau. Beth would like to say chi miigwich (thank you very much) to Ozaawaabik for sharing these teachings.

Great Lakes Inter-Tribal Council (GLITC) Native American Tobacco Network Director Teresa K. Barber says that in her Ojibwe and Oneida teachings, her parents had them put down tobacco whenever they harvested any plants or foods. "When we went on trips, we put it down for safe travels. When we use our tobacco, we use it for asking help for others." She was also taught that when a storm is approaching, to put tobacco down. "We believe that Nature has to happen, so when the storm comes, we put it down to protect us, but also to do the job it has to do. I've given it for my Oneida and my Ojibwe name. We also practice tobacco burning ceremonies and we use it to put it in sacred fires."

Wayne "Minogiizhig" Valliere, Lac du Flambeau tribal member, states: "Tobacco was given to us to offer to the spirit world, for harvesting a deer or a fish or a plant from the forest. Tobacco was given to us to respect all living things. It wasn't given to us for self-gratification." (Interview with Steve Busalacchi/Health First Wisconsin, January 2012)

How to Grow Your Own Tobacco

You can obtain tobacco seeds from: family, friends, community members, spiritual leaders, medicine people, possibly at pow wows or traditional ceremonies, or by contacting Wisconsin Native American Tobacco Network Director Teresa K. Barber at GLITC. (tbardber@glitc.org)

Supplies needed for growing tobacco:
• Traditional tobacco seeds
• Potting soil
• 12-20 oz. disposable cups (clear preferred)
• Clear plastic wrap
• Rubber bands
• Spray bottle filled with water
• Scissors
• Good thoughts

We are sharing instructions on how to grow tobacco from the lessons we have been taught. However, we recognize that each Tribal community is different and may have different protocols, prohibitions, and instructions for growing tobacco. We encourage you to check with your community elders for guidance, and adjust our instructions as needed.

Tobacco's Present

Traditional tobacco needs a temperature of between 65-80 degrees Fahrenheit and light in order to germinate, or transform from a seed to a seedling. The temperature and light requirements, along with our short growing season in the Great Lake region, make traditional tobacco difficult to begin outside. For this reason, the instructions that follow help you make a "mini-greenhouse" to start your seeds indoors.

There are various rules of thumb about when to start your seeds. Some say to plant tobacco after the thunders arrive in the spring (after the first thunderstorm); others say to plant the week before the March full moon.

To make your mini-greenhouse, take the disposable cup and fill it about half to two-thirds full of potting soil. It's good to use potting soil instead of dirt, because potting soil has been treated so it won't have bugs, disease, or weeds in it. Sprinkle five to eight seeds on top of the potting soil in the cup, spacing them to allow each room to grow. Tobacco seeds are very small, so estimating five to eight seeds is much easier than actually counting them out. Do not bury the seeds under the dirt as they need light to germinate. Use a spray bottle to spray the seeds with a light mist to water them. Make sure you spray enough water to make the soil wet. Cut a square of plastic wrap large enough to cover the cup with about an inch or more around the entire edge. Place the plastic wrap over the cup and secure it with a rubber band. Place the cup in a warm sunny area, or use a grow light. Make sure the soil stays moist, uncovering it and spraying as needed to keep it moist, but not drenched, since too much water can harm the roots.

The seeds take about ten days to germinate (change from a seed to a seedling). Uncover the cup if the seedlings grow to the height the plastic covering. Once the seedlings reach about six inches in height they can be transplanted outside when the soil has warmed and all danger of frost

has passed. Dig a hole where each tobacco plant will be placed (tobacco plants like sunny areas). If you want to fertilize you can place fish guts or fish heads at the bottom of the hole, or use a liquid organic fertilizer. Carefully remove the plants from the cup and gently separate them from each other, being careful not to disturb the root structures. Place a plant with roots in the hole and fill around the plant with potting soil to stabilize and support it. Water generously to ensure the roots take hold. Tobacco uses a lot of nutrients to grow. So each year you should rotate where you place the tobacco. If rotating is not an option, make sure you fertilize well. Water every few days at first to help the roots establish themselves, then water weekly—or more often during a hot, dry spell.

The plant will flower eventually. Flower buds will grow at the tops of the plant. When this happens, some people trim off the flower buds so the plant will focus its energy on growing leaves. The flower buds are where the seeds come from in the harvesting stage, so if you want seeds to plant next year, do not cut them off. The flower petals will fall and pods containing seeds will take form.

About five to seven weeks after flowering tobacco is ready to harvest. The leaves will mature from the bottom to the top. The leaves will turn from green to yellow and begin to dry out. The leaves can be picked as they ripen, or you can pull the whole plant up when the seed pods ripen and pull all the leaves off at one time. If you would like to get seeds and save them for next year, wait to harvest the plant until the seedpods crack. You can collect the seeds by placing the seed pods in a bag and shaking to release the seeds. To save the seeds until the next year, place them in the freezer, or keep them dry in a paper envelope or bag, until you are ready to plant them and repeat the cycle.

To cure the tobacco leaves, hang them to dry indoors. Do not hang the leaves near a heat source or they will cure too fast. The slower the curing process, the better. Leaves can take four weeks to a year to cure.

Guiding Principles of Tobacco Use

1. Always use with positive thoughts and feelings.
2. Try to use only traditional tobacco (if available).
3. Hold in your left hand, as this is the arm closest to your heart.
4. Do not use while under the influence of drugs or alcohol.
5. Make sure to let the person or persons know your request before handing them your tobacco, so they have the right to respectively decline, if need be.

Health Impacts of Commercial Tobacco

Commercial tobacco (*Nicotiana tabacum*), which is commercially manufactured, contains many carcinogens (cancer-causing chemicals), including:

1.) Naphthalene (mothballs)
2.) Arsenic (rat poison)
3.) Hexamine (ingredient in explosives)
4.) Carbon Monoxide (car exhaust)
5.) Ammonia (household cleaner)
6.) Nitrous oxide (car power booster)
7.) Benzene (gasoline additive)
8.) Butane (cigarette lighter fluid)
9.) Acrolein (pesticide)
10.) Acetone (nail polish remover)

Commercial tobacco is related to the history of colonization in our country. The American Indian population has suffered from colonization which brought with it, among other things, removal from traditional lands, relocation, confinement to reservations, forced boarding school attendance, attempts at forced assimilation, termination of federal recognition of Tribes, termination of trust responsibility, and near genocide. This has created a severe loss of culture, which may have led to the great disparity in health between American Indians and the general population, and contributed to their use of commercial tobacco. According to The People's Theory of the Cultural Wellness Center, "individualism, loss of culture, and loss of community make you sick" (Cultural Wellness Center, 2004, formerly Powderhorn/Phillips Cultural Wellness Center). This "sickness" is evidenced in the rates and effects of tobacco abuse among American Indians. Native Americans have higher rates of tobacco misuse (at 33.4%), and begin smoking at an earlier age than other ethnic groups (Maurice et al., 2005; Levin et al., 2002). Caucasians come in second at 22.2%, African Americans at a rate of 20.2%, Hispanics 15%, and Asian/Pacific Islanders at a rate of 11.3% (Maurice, et al., 2005). In the Great Lakes region, 44.1% of American Indians are reported to be current smokers (Denny et al., 2003).

Problems from smoking occur disproportionately in the American Indian community as well. Four of the five leading causes of death among American Indians in Wisconsin are related to tobacco misuse (cancer, coronary heart disease, diabetes, and chronic lower respiratory disease) (Great Lakes Inter-Tribal Epidemiology Center, 2010). American Indians in Wisconsin have higher cancer rates than people of other ethnicities in the state once you adjust for age. The increased rate of cancer is in large part due to a much greater lung cancer rate (Indian Health Service, 2004).

Research on smoking prevalence among American Indian youth mirrors adult use with American Indian youth having the highest prevalence. According to the 2003 National Survey of Drug Use & Health, the past month smoking prevalence rate for youth ages 12-17 by ethnicity is American Indian/Alaska Native 23.1%, White 14.9%, Hispanic or Latino 9.3%, Black or African American 6.5%, and Asian at 4.3% (Gfroerer & Caraballo, 2006). Research on several reservations and areas near reservations in 2004 found that 63% of American Indian youth have tried smoking and 12% smoke daily (Beauvais et al., 2007). Research at an American Indian event in

Canada found that 32% of youth (aged 12 to 22) currently smoke cigarettes (Ritchie & Reading, 2003).

Comparing urban versus rural/reservation smoking prevalence rates, there appears to be no difference; differences may exist in the types of tobacco used abusively. During a study in California, Jennifer Unger and colleagues found no significant difference in smoking prevalence between rural and urban American Indian youth, with smoking rates of 29.3% and 27.7% respectively (2003). Likewise, during a study in the Southwest, Yu and colleagues found no significant difference in cigarette smoking prevalence (ever used) between rural and urban American Indian youth, with smoking rates of 64% and 55% respectively (2005).

The Wisconsin Native Youth Tobacco Survey, conducted in 2008, determined rates of tobacco use among Native communities in Wisconsin (GLITEC, 2008). The survey asked tribal youth of middle and high school age questions about perception, attitudes, knowledge about traditional tobacco and commercial tobacco use. It is the first ever statewide Native Youth Tobacco Survey addressing these issues, and over 1,800 American Indian/Alaska Native (AI/AN) representing all Wisconsin tribal communities were surveyed. Survey results (see Table 1 below) show that Wisconsin American Indian/Alaska Native (AI/AN) youth have higher smoking rates compared to all other races in Wisconsin, and are more exposed to environmental (secondhand) smoke.

Table 1: Wisconsin Native Youth Tobacco Survey Results: Aggregate Data	Middle School		High School	
	AI/AN %	WI All Races %	AI/AN %	WI All Races %
Prevalence				
Ever tried cigarette smoking	43.0	16.4	69.6	47.2
Smoked cigarettes during last month	16.8	4.3	38.2	20.7
Environmental Tobacco Smoke (ETS)				
Exposed during last week	71.2	43.4	78.5	59.0
Think that ETS is harmful	89.2	93.2	91.7	95.5
Media, School, and Community				
Seen commercials about dangers of tobacco during last month	57.9	60.7	66.1	77.3
Learned about dangers of tobacco during school year	52.3	69.2	33.6	43.6
Participated in community events to discourage tobacco abuse during past year	19.2	8.6	16.1	8.4
Access and Availability				
Take from store or family member	22.0	23.5	6.5	Unavailable
Gave money to someone else to buy	30.3	32.3	37.2	38.1

The Wisconsin Native Youth Tobacco Survey results also demonstrate that use of traditional tobacco (versus cigarettes or other forms of tobacco abuse) for ceremonial or spiritual purposes is associated with lower rates of commercial tobacco initiation, and commercial tobacco use within the past 30 days.

Previous research has also shown us that the majority of smokers start smoking before their 18th birthday (Mowery et al., 2000). This statistic, combined with the fact that American Indian youth begin smoking earlier than their non-Indian counterparts, and have more serious health effects from smoking, give rise to a great need to create smoking interventions for American Indian youth.

Harms of Commercial Tobacco Abuse and Quitting Tips

The following information on the harms of commercial tobacco and on smoking cessation was submitted by Mark Caskey, Menominee Nation Wellness Director.

Tobacco abuse is the single greatest cause of preventable death globally. Tobacco abuse leads most commonly to diseases affecting the heart and lungs, with smoking being a major risk factor for heart attacks, strokes, chronic obstructive pulmonary disease (COPD) including emphysema and cancer (particularly lung cancer, cancers of the larynx and mouth, and pancreatic cancer).

Mortality
- Overall life expectance is reduced with estimates ranging from 10 to 17.9 years fewer than non-smokers.
- In the United States alone, cigarette smoking and exposure to tobacco smoke accounts for roughly one in five, or at least 443,000 premature deaths annually.
- "In the United States alone, tobacco kills the equivalent of three jumbo jets full of people crashing every day, with no survivors, 365 days of the year." -ABC's Peter Jennings

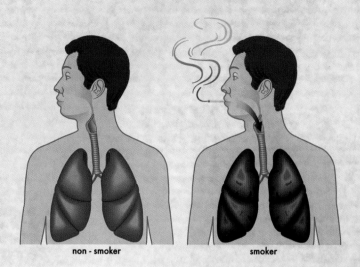

non - smoker   smoker

- Wisconsin, Michigan, and Minnesota tribes have the highest rate of lung cancer mortality when compared with tribes throughout the U.S. Historically, lung cancer was considered to be a rare disease in Wisconsin Native Americans.
- In one Wisconsin Tribe, lung cancer rates went up by 195% in the last fifteen years.
- 90% of lung cancers are caused by commercial tobacco abuse.
- Half of the people who can't quit die of a smoking related illness.
- Smokers use the health care system 50% more than non-smokers.

Heart disease used to be the number one killer in Wisconsin Tribes. Now it is cancer, with lung cancer being the number one type of cancer in some Wisconsin Tribes. The number one preventable cause of both heart disease and lung cancer is commercial tobacco abuse.
- Why do Wisconsin Native Americans die of lung cancer? Because the tar in smoke damages lung tissue.
- Why? Because the person smoked a long time.
- Why? Because of addiction, psychological and social reasons, and habit.
- Why? Because powerful tobacco companies know ways to market commercial tobacco that can cause Native people to become addicted.
- Why? Because of a more lenient attitude toward smoking on the Rez.

Recreational use of commercial tobacco is killing OUR PEOPLE!

Tobacco's Present

Disease and Consequences of Secondhand Smoke

Secondhand smoke is a mixture of smoke from the burning end of a cigarette, pipe or cigar, and the smoke exhaled from the lungs of smokers. It contains more than 7,000 chemicals, including hundreds that are toxic and about 70 that can cause cancer. It is involuntarily inhaled, and lingers in the air hours after cigarettes have been extinguished. It can cause a wide range of adverse health effects, including cancer, respiratory infections and asthma. Non-smokers who are exposed to secondhand smoke at home or work increase their heart disease risk by 25–30% and their lung cancer risk by 20–30%. Secondhand smoke has been estimated to cause 38,000 deaths per year, of which 3,400 are deaths from lung cancer in non-smokers.

There are no safe levels of exposure to secondhand smoke, and there is no available adequate ventilation technology based upon scientific studies that can ensure the protection and prevention of secondhand smoke health-related illnesses. Everyone has the right to breathe clean air and be free from the pollution caused by commercial tobacco products.

Effects of Thirdhand Smoke

Thirdhand smoke is generally considered to be residual nicotine and other chemicals left on a variety of indoor surfaces by commercial tobacco smoke. This residue is thought to react with common indoor pollutants to create a toxic mix. This toxic mix of thirdhand smoke contains cancer-causing substances, posing a potential health hazard to nonsmokers who are exposed to it, especially children.

Studies show that thirdhand smoke clings to hair, skin, clothes, furniture, drapes, walls, bedding, carpets, dust, vehicles and other surfaces, even long after smoking has stopped. Infants, children and nonsmoking adults may be at risk of tobacco-related health problems when they inhale, ingest or touch substances containing thirdhand smoke. Thirdhand smoke is a relatively new concept, and researchers are still studying its possible dangers.

Thirdhand smoke residue builds up on surfaces over time and resists normal cleaning. Thirdhand smoke can't be eliminated by airing out rooms, opening windows, using fans or air conditioners, or confining smoking to only certain areas of a home. Thirdhand smoke remains long after smoking has stopped.

Children ingest twice the amount of dust that grown-ups do. Let's say a grown-up weighs 150 pounds (68 kilograms). Let's say a baby weighs 15 pounds (seven kilograms). The infant ingests twice the dust, due to faster respiration and proximity to dusty surfaces. Effectively, they'll get 20 times the exposure to thirdhand smoke compared to an adult.

The only way to protect nonsmokers from thirdhand smoke is to create a smoke-free environment, whether that's your private home or vehicle, or in public places, such as casinos, hotels and restaurants.

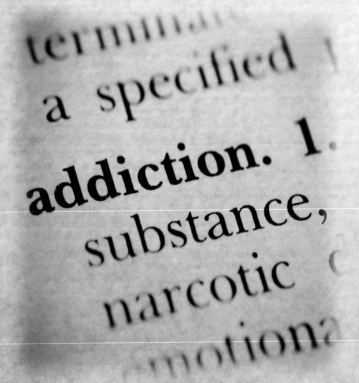

Commercial
TOBACCO USE

Surrounds her with toxins and disease.

Tobacco's Present

RESTORING TRADITION AND REDUCING HARMS

Pregnancy and Smoking

If a pregnant woman smokes, her blood and therefore her child's blood will contain less oxygen than normal. This can cause the fetal heart rate to rise as baby struggles to get enough oxygen.

The particles in tobacco smoke contain different toxic substances that change the blood's ability to work in a healthy and normal manner. This can affect the placenta that feeds the baby.

Babies born to mothers who smoke: are more likely to be born prematurely and with a low birth weight, have organs that are smaller, and have poorer lung function.

Mother Earth is Not an Ashtray

Everything -- absolutely everything – about cigarettes can threaten life on our beloved planet. They pollute the ground we walk on and the air we breathe. And if we smoke, cigarettes poison us slowly, stealing our quality of life long before they kill us.

In fact, cigarettes are the most littered item in America and the world. Cigarette filters are made of cellulose acetate, not cotton, and they can take decades to degrade. Not only does cigarette litter ruin even the most picturesque setting, but the toxic residue in cigarette filters is damaging to the environment. Toxin-filled cigarette butts work their way into our waterways, primarily through storm drains that dump into streams and lakes.

Careless Smoking

Smoking causes about 10% of the global burden of fire deaths, and smokers are placed at an increased risk of injury-related deaths in general, partly due to experiencing an increased risk of dying in a motor vehicle crash.

Forest Fires

Discarded cigarette butts pose a significant threat to our environment in terms of fire. Every year, forest fires ravage vast areas, killing off wildlife and vegetation that take years to return. According to the National Fire Protection Agency, upwards of 90,000 fires every year in the United States alone are caused by cigarettes. Cigarette-induced fires claim hundreds of lives in the United States each year, and injure thousands more, not

24

to mention the millions of dollars that go up in smoke in property damage.

Commercial Tobacco and Addiction

Tobacco abuse is really a brain disease. Whether smoked or chewed, nicotine is one of the most highly addictive drugs used in today's society. And once you're hooked, it's extremely hard to overcome this addiction. Surveys have shown that most adult smokers first tried cigarettes during their teen years, and there is a direct relationship between early smoking and adult addiction. Nicotine withdrawal symptoms may include craving, irritability, insomnia, headache, anxiety, depression, and impaired concentration.

Treating Tobacco Dependence

Only 5% of smokers are able to quit for good by going cold turkey. Effective treatments exist. Native American smokers trying to quit, except in the presence of special circumstances, should consider receiving pharmacotherapy for smoking cessation. Why? Because there is less discomfort when going through quitting process, and it increases your chance of successful quitting.

It also buys you some "healthy time" while you're incorporating behavioral changes.

Tobacco Abuse Counseling

Where do you get support for quitting? Talk to your Tobacco Treatment Specialist. Adding counseling to medication increases success of quitting by 70%. Most tobacco abuse treatment counseling today consists of spending five minutes to help you for the rest of your life. You need to spend time with your tobacco treatment specialist so they can know your story and help you quit and stay quit. No client and treatment are alike, and your counselor can help you with a quit plan that's a good fit for you.

Counseling is like using a windshield wiper so you can see the road and drive ahead safely. Your counselor will work with you, and will walk beside you, not in front of you. They can give you resources and not a lot of rules; can give you empathy and not sympathy. You're the expert and in charge of your own plan. They can help you to learn new skills to respond to old temptations.

Tobacco's Future

We have tried our best to share our story of tobacco with you. We hope that after reading this document, you now have a strong understanding of how important traditional tobacco is, and how devastating commercial tobacco is in our American Indian communities. Earlier we mentioned the People's Theory from the Cultural Wellness Center. Their theory's downward process says that as you lose your culture, you lose your health. This is very apparent in our relationship with tobacco. As we lost our culture, we lost our knowledge of traditional tobacco because of government policies that prohibited our practice of Native religion, and many of us shifted towards using commercial tobacco, both ceremonially and recreationally. As a result, we are losing our health, suffering, and dying much earlier from commercial tobacco related illnesses.

The People's Theory also has an upward process, which states that as you gain your culture, you gain health. We can achieve better health by shifting back to the use of traditional tobacco in our ceremonies while eliminating commercial tobacco from our lives and communities. We can do this by reaching out to people who grow traditional tobacco in our communities and by growing it ourselves. We seek a future where commercial tobacco is not a part of us. We seek a future where our culture is preserved and honored. We seek a future where our communities and future generations are safe…happy…and healthy… Wouldn't that be a great story? We are all in control of this story's ending. Please ask yourself, where are you in this story and what ending will you help to realize?

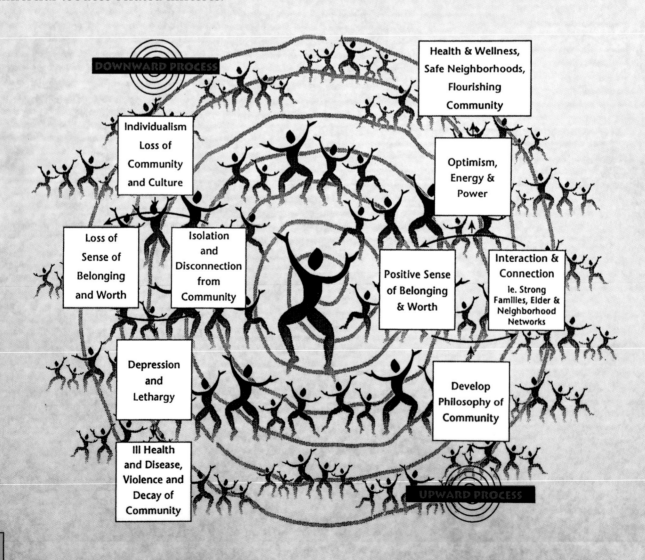

REFERENCES

American Indian Community Tobacco Project (2006). Tobacco: Telling Our Story, p.13.

American Indian Religious Freedom Act, Pub.L. 95-341, § Aug. 11, 1978, 92 Stat. 469, codified as amended at 42 U.S.C. § 1996 (1996).   Retrieved October 31, 2012 at http://www.law.cornell.edu/uscode/text/42/1996.

American Lung Association (2004). Smoking and American Indians/Alaska Native Fact Sheet. American Lung Association. American Lung Association, 2004. Retrieved December 2006 from http://www.lungusa.org/site/apps/s/content.asp?c=dvLUK9O0E&b=34706&ct=3052551.

Beauvais, F., P. Jumper Thurman, M. Burnside, and B. Plested, 2007. "Prevalence of American Indian Adolescent Tobacco Use: 1993-2004." Substance Use & Misuse 42 (2007): 591-601.

Brokenleg, Isaiah (2006). Exploring the Unraveling Hoop: Tobacco Use, Abuse, and Tobacco Abuse Predictive Factors among Urban American Indian Youth in the Twin Cities. Retrieved October 28, 2120 at http://www.aictp.umn.edu/docs/AICTPBrokenlegYouthReport.pdf

Cultural Wellness Center (2004, formerly the Powderhorn Phillips Cultural Center). Moving Ahead with Experience Based Knowledge to Heal Communities Annual Report 2004.   Cultural Wellness Center, Minneapolis.

Denny, C., D. Holtzman, and N. Cobb (2003). "Surveillance for Health Behaviors of American Indians and Alaska Natives: Findings from the Behavioral Risk Factor Surveillance System, 1997-2000." Morbidity and Mortality Weekly Report 52 (2003). 11 July 2007 <http://www.cdc.gov/mmwr/PDF/ss/ss5207.pdf>.

Great Lakes Inter-Tribal Epidemiology Center (2010). Community Health Data Profile: Michigan, Minnesota, and Wisconsin Tribal Communities 2010. Lac du Flambeau: Great Lakes Inter-Tribal Council, Inc.

Great Lakes Inter-Tribal Epidemiology Center (2008). Native Youth Tobacco Survey, 2008. Lac du Flambeau: Great Lakes Inter-Tribal Council, Inc.

Gfroerer, J., and R. Caraballo (2006). "Racial/Ethnic Differences among Youths in Cigarette Smoking and Susceptibility to Start Smoking --- United States, 2002-2004." Morbidity and Mortality Weekly Report 55 21 July 2007. <http://www.cdc.gov/mmwr/preview/mmwrhtml/mm5547a4.htm>.

Indian Health Service (2004). Regional Differences in Indian Health: 2000-2001. Department of Health and Human Services, Rockville, MD.

Levin, S., V. L. Welch, R. A. Bell, and M. L. Casper (2002). "Geographic Variation in Cardiovascular Disease Risk Factors among American Indians and Comparisons with the Corresponding State Populations." Ethnic Health 7.

Maurice, E., A. Trosclair, R. Merritt, R. Caraballo, A. Malarcher, C. Husten, and T. Pechacek (2005). "Cigarette Smoking Among Adults---United States, 2004." Morbidity and Mortality Weekly Report 54 Retrieved July 10, 2007 from http://www.cdc.gov/mmwr/preview/mmwrhtml/mm5444a2.htm

McGaa, E. (1990) Mother Earth Spirituality Native American Paths to Healing Ourselves and Our World. 1st Ed. San Francisco: Harper & Row.

REFERENCES

Mowery, P. D., P. D. Brink, and M. C. Farrelly (2000). Legacy First Look Report 3 Pathways to Established Smoking: Results From the 1999 National Youth Tobacco Survey. American Legacy Foundation. Washington D.C.: American Legacy Foundation.

Oneida Nation of Wisconsin website, "Oneida Creation Story." Retrieved Oct. 29, 2012 from http://www.oneidanation.org/culture/page.aspx?id=1278

Ritchie, A., and J. Reading (2003). "Tobacco Smoking Status among Aboriginal Youth." Circumpolar Health, 405-409.

Struthers, R., and F. S. Hodge (2004). "Sacred Tobacco
Use in Ojibwe Communities." Journal of Holistic Nursing 22.3, 209-225.

Turtle Mountain Chippewa Historical Society Website, "Mashkiki." Content provided by Kade M. Ferris, M.S. Retrieved October 1, 2012 from http://www.chippewaheritage.com/1/post/2012/03/four-sacred-medicines-muskiiki.html

US Centers for Disease Control (2012). "Secondhand Smoke (SHS) Facts." Retrieved October 29, 2012 from http://www.cdc.gov/tobacco/data_statistics/fact_sheets/secondhand_smoke/general_facts/

Winter, J. C. Tobacco Use by Native Americans. Norman, OK: University of Oklahoma P, 2000.

Yu, M., A. Rubin Stiffman, and S. Freedenthal (2005). "Factors Affecting American Indian Adolescent Tobacco Use." Addictive Behaviors 30, 889-904.

Wikipedia.org (2012) Anishinaabe traditional beliefs. Retrieved October 31, 2012, from http://en.wikipedia.org/wiki/Anishinaabe_traditional_beliefs#Nanabozho_stories

Wikepedia.org (2012) "Civilian Conservation Corps," Retrieved Oct. 29, 2012 from http://en.wikipedia.org/wiki/Civilian_Conservation_Corps